This Recipe Book belongs to:

_____

_____

_____

Table of Contents

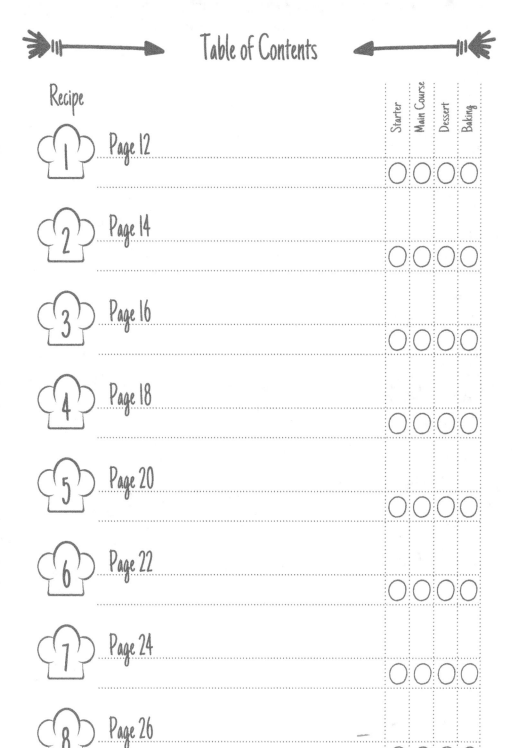

Table of Contents

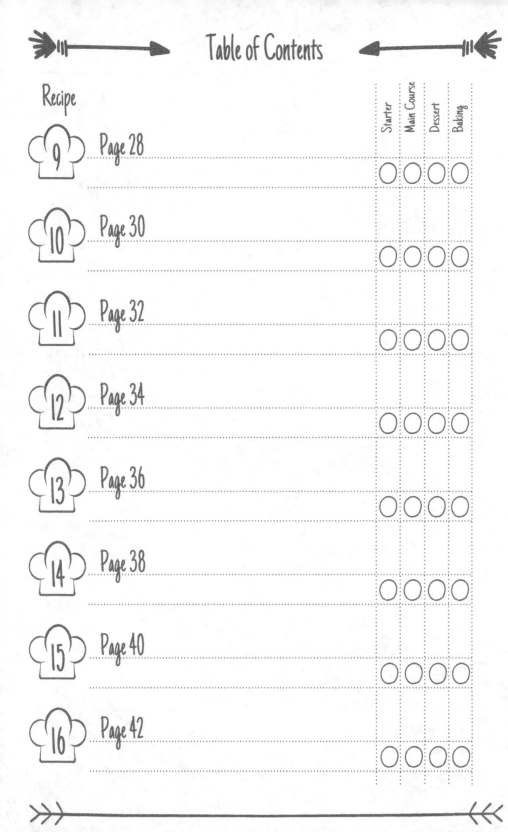

Table of Contents

Table of Contents

 # Table of Contents

Table of Contents

Table of Contents

Table of Contents

EATING IS A
necessity
BUT COOKING
is an art.

Name: ....

Date: .... **Source:** ....

○ Starter ○ Main Course ○ Dessert ○ Baking

Servings: .... **Prep Time:** .... **Cook Time:** ....

Difficulty: ○ ○ ○ ○ ○

Ingredients

....

....

....

....

....

....

....

....

Personal Notes:

Directions:

....

....

....

....

....

....

....

....

....

....

Rating: ⛑ ⛑ ⛑ ⛑ ⛑

Personal Notes:

2 Name:

Date: .... Source: ....

○ Starter ○ Main Course ○ Dessert ○ Baking

Servings: .... Prep Time: .... Cook Time: ....

Difficulty: ○ ○ ○ ○ ○

Ingredients

....

....

....

....

....

....

....

....

....

Personal Notes:

Directions:

Rating: ♟ ♟ ♟ ♟ ♟

Personal Notes:

3 Name: ....

Date: .... Source: ....

○ Starter ○ Main Course ○ Dessert ○ Baking

Servings: .... Prep Time: .... Cook Time: ....

Difficulty: ○ ○ ○ ○ ○

Ingredients

....
....
....
....
....
....
....
....
....

Personal Notes:

Directions:

Rating: 🎩 🎩 🎩 🎩 🎩

Personal Notes:

4 Name:

Date: .... Source: ....

○ Starter ○ Main Course ○ Dessert ○ Baking

Servings: .... Prep Time: .... Cook Time: ....

Difficulty: ○ ○ ○ ○ ○

Ingredients

....

....

....

....

....

....

....

....

Personal Notes:

Directions:

....

....

....

....

....

....

....

....

....

....

....

Rating:

Personal Notes:

5 Name:

Date: .... Source: ....

○ Starter ○ Main Course ○ Dessert ○ Baking

Servings: .... Prep Time: .... Cook Time: ....

Difficulty: ○ ○ ○ ○ ○

Ingredients

....

....

....

....

....

....

....

....

Personal Notes:

Directions:

....

....

....

....

....

....

....

....

....

....

Rating: ♔ ♔ ♔ ♔ ♔

Personal Notes:

6 Name:

Date: .... Source: ....

○ Starter ○ Main Course ○ Dessert ○ Baking

Servings: .... Prep Time: .... Cook Time: ....

Difficulty: ○ ○ ○ ○ ○

Ingredients

....

....

....

....

....

....

....

....

Personal Notes:

Directions:

....

....

....

....

....

....

....

....

....

....

....

Rating:

Personal Notes:

7 Name: ....

Date: .... Source: ....

○ Starter ○ Main Course ○ Dessert ○ Baking

Servings: .... Prep Time: .... Cook Time: ....

Difficulty: ○ ○ ○ ○ ○

Ingredients

....
....
....
....
....
....
....
....

Personal Notes:

Directions:

....

....

....

....

....

....

....

....

....

....

....

Rating: 🎩 🎩 🎩 🎩 🎩

Personal Notes:

8 Name:

Date: .... Source: ....

○ Starter   ○ Main Course   ○ Dessert   ○ Baking

Servings: .... Prep Time: .... Cook Time: ....

Difficulty: ○   ○   ○   ○   ○

Ingredients

....

....

....

....

....

....

....

....

Personal Notes:

Directions:

....

....

....

....

....

....

....

....

....

....

Rating: ♟ ♟ ♟ ♟ ♟

Personal Notes:

9 Name: ....

Date: .... Source: ....

○ Starter   ○ Main Course   ○ Dessert   ○ Baking

Servings: .... Prep Time: .... Cook Time: ....

Difficulty: ○ ○ ○ ○ ○

Ingredients

....
....
....
....
....
....
....
....

Personal Notes:

Directions:

Rating:

Personal Notes:

10 Name:

Date: .... Source: ....

○ Starter ○ Main Course ○ Dessert ○ Baking

Servings: .... Prep Time: .... Cook Time: ....

Difficulty: ○ ○ ○ ○ ○

Ingredients

....

....

....

....

....

....

....

....

Personal Notes:

Directions:

....

....

....

....

....

....

....

....

....

....

....

....

Rating: ♟ ♟ ♟ ♟ ♟

Personal Notes:

Name:

Date: .... Source: ....

○ Starter ○ Main Course ○ Dessert ○ Baking

Servings: .... Prep Time: .... Cook Time: ....

Difficulty: ○ ○ ○ ○ ○

Ingredients

....
....
....
....
....
....
....
....

Personal Notes:

Directions:

Rating: 🍳 🍳 🍳 🍳 🍳

Personal Notes:

12 Name:

Date: ....   Source: ....

○ Starter ○ Main Course ○ Dessert ○ Baking

Servings: .... Prep Time: .... Cook Time: ....

Difficulty: ○ ○ ○ ○ ○

Ingredients

....
....
....
....
....
....
....
....

Personal Notes:

Directions:

....

....

....

....

....

....

....

....

....

....

Rating: ♙ ♙ ♙ ♙ ♙

Personal Notes:

13 Name: ....

Date: .... Source: ....

○ Starter ○ Main Course ○ Dessert ○ Baking

Servings: .... Prep Time: .... Cook Time: ....

Difficulty: ○ ○ ○ ○ ○

Ingredients

....

....

....

....

....

....

....

....

Personal Notes:

Directions:

....

....

....

....

....

....

....

....

....

....

....

Rating:

Personal Notes:

14 Name: ....

Date: .... Source: ....

◯ Starter ◯ Main Course ◯ Dessert ◯ Baking

Servings: .... Prep Time: .... Cook Time: ....

Difficulty: ◯   ◯   ◯   ◯   ◯

Ingredients

....

....

....

....

....

....

....

....

Personal Notes:

Directions:

Rating: ♙ ♙ ♙ ♙ ♙

Personal Notes:

15 Name:

Date: .... Source: ....

○ Starter ○ Main Course ○ Dessert ○ Baking

Servings: .... Prep Time: .... Cook Time: ....

Difficulty: ○ ○ ○ ○ ○

Ingredients

....

....

....

....

....

....

....

....

Personal Notes:

Directions:

Rating: 🎩 🎩 🎩 🎩 🎩

Personal Notes:

16 Name:

Date: .... Source: ....

○ Starter ○ Main Course ○ Dessert ○ Baking

Servings: .... Prep Time: .... Cook Time: ....

Difficulty: ○ ○ ○ ○ ○

Ingredients

....

....

....

....

....

....

....

....

Personal Notes:

Directions:

....

....

....

....

....

....

....

....

....

....

Rating: ♙ ♙ ♙ ♙ ♙

Personal Notes:

17 Name:

Date: .... Source: ....

○ Starter ○ Main Course ○ Dessert ○ Baking

Servings: .... Prep Time: .... Cook Time: ....

Difficulty: ○ ○ ○ ○ ○

Ingredients

....
....
....
....
....
....
....
....

Personal Notes:

Directions:
....

....

....

....

....

....

....

....

....

....

Rating:

Personal Notes:

18 Name: ....

Date: .... Source: ....

○ Starter ○ Main Course ○ Dessert ○ Baking

Servings: .... Prep Time: .... Cook Time: ....

Difficulty: ○ ○ ○ ○ ○

Ingredients

....

....

....

....

....

....

....

....

Personal Notes:

Directions:

....

....

....

....

....

....

....

....

....

....

....

Rating: ♟ ♟ ♟ ♟ ♟

Personal Notes:

19 Name: ....

Date: .... Source: ....

◯ Starter ◯ Main Course ◯ Dessert ◯ Baking

Servings: .... Prep Time: .... Cook Time: ....

Difficulty: ◯   ◯   ◯   ◯   ◯

Ingredients

....
....
....
....
....
....
....
....

Personal Notes:

Directions:

....

....

....

....

....

....

....

....

....

....

....

Rating: ♙ ♙ ♙ ♙ ♙

Personal Notes:

20 Name: ....

Date: .... Source: ....

○ Starter ○ Main Course ○ Dessert ○ Baking

Servings: .... Prep Time: .... Cook Time: ....

Difficulty: ○   ○   ○   ○   ○

Ingredients

....

....

....

....

....

....

....

....

Personal Notes:

Directions:

Rating: ♟ ♟ ♟ ♟ ♟

Personal Notes:

21 Name: ....

Date: .... Source: ....

○ Starter   ○ Main Course   ○ Dessert   ○ Baking

Servings: .... Prep Time: .... Cook Time: ....

Difficulty: ○   ○   ○   ○   ○

Ingredients

....	....	....	....
....	....	....	....
....	....	....	....
....	....	....	....
....	....	....	....
....	....	....	....
....	....	....	....
....	....	....	....

Personal Notes:

Directions:

....
....
....
....
....
....
....
....
....
....

Rating:

Personal Notes:

22 Name: ....

Date: .... Source: ....

○ Starter ○ Main Course ○ Dessert ○ Baking

Servings: .... Prep Time: .... Cook Time: ....

Difficulty: ○   ○   ○   ○   ○

Ingredients

....	....	....	....
....	....	....	....
....	....	....	....
....	....	....	....
....	....	....	....
....	....	....	....
....	....	....	....
....	....	....	....

Personal Notes:

Directions:

....
....
....
....
....
....
....
....
....
....
....

Rating: 🧑‍🍳 🧑‍🍳 🧑‍🍳 🧑‍🍳 🧑‍🍳

Personal Notes:

23 Name:

Date: .... Source: ....

○ Starter ○ Main Course ○ Dessert ○ Baking

Servings: .... Prep Time: .... Cook Time: ....

Difficulty: ○ ○ ○ ○ ○

Ingredients

....
....
....
....
....
....
....
....
....

Personal Notes:

Directions:

....

....

....

....

....

....

....

....

....

....

....

Rating:

Personal Notes:

24 Name:

Date: .... Source: ....

◯ Starter   ◯ Main Course   ◯ Dessert   ◯ Baking

Servings: .... Prep Time: .... Cook Time: ....

Difficulty: ◯ ◯ ◯ ◯ ◯

Ingredients

....

....

....

....

....

....

....

....

....

Personal Notes:

Directions:

....

....

....

....

....

....

....

....

....

....

....

Rating: 🎩 🎩 🎩 🎩 🎩

Personal Notes:

25 Name: ....

Date: .... Source: ....

○ Starter ○ Main Course ○ Dessert ○ Baking

Servings: .... Prep Time: .... Cook Time: ....

Difficulty: ○ ○ ○ ○ ○

Ingredients

....

....

....

....

....

....

....

....

Personal Notes:

Directions:

....

....

....

....

....

....

....

....

....

....

....

....

Rating:

Personal Notes:

26 Name: ....

Date: .... Source: ....

○ Starter ○ Main Course ○ Dessert ○ Baking

Servings: .... Prep Time: .... Cook Time: ....

Difficulty: ○ ○ ○ ○ ○

Ingredients

....

....

....

....

....

....

....

....

....

Personal Notes:

Directions:

....

....

....

....

....

....

....

....

....

....

Rating:

Personal Notes:

27 Name: ....

Date: .... Source: ....

○ Starter ○ Main Course ○ Dessert ○ Baking

Servings: .... Prep Time: .... Cook Time: ....

Difficulty: ○ ○ ○ ○ ○

Ingredients

....

....

....

....

....

....

....

....

....

Personal Notes:

Directions:

....
....
....
....
....
....
....
....
....
....
....

Rating: ♟ ♟ ♟ ♟ ♟

Personal Notes:

28 Name:

Date: .... Source: ....

○ Starter ○ Main Course ○ Dessert ○ Baking

Servings: .... Prep Time: .... Cook Time: ....

Difficulty: ○   ○   ○   ○   ○

Ingredients

....

....

....

....

....

....

....

....

Personal Notes:

Directions:

....

....

....

....

....

....

....

....

....

....

....

Rating: 🍳 🍳 🍳 🍳 🍳

Personal Notes:

29 Name: ....

Date: .... Source: ....

○ Starter ○ Main Course ○ Dessert ○ Baking

Servings: .... Prep Time: .... Cook Time: ....

Difficulty: ○ ○ ○ ○ ○

Ingredients

....

....

....

....

....

....

....

....

Personal Notes:

Directions:

....

....

....

....

....

....

....

....

....

....

Rating:

Personal Notes:

30 Name:

Date: .... Source: ....

○ Starter ○ Main Course ○ Dessert ○ Baking

Servings: .... Prep Time: .... Cook Time: ....

Difficulty: ○ ○ ○ ○ ○

Ingredients

....	....	....	....
....	....	....	....
....	....	....	....
....	....	....	....
....	....	....	....
....	....	....	....
....	....	....	....
....	....	....	....
....	....	....	....

Personal Notes:

Directions:

....

....

....

....

....

....

....

....

....

....

....

....

Rating:

Personal Notes:

31 Name: ....

Date: .... Source: ....

○ Starter ○ Main Course ○ Dessert ○ Baking

Servings: .... Prep Time: .... Cook Time: ....

Difficulty: ○ ○ ○ ○ ○

Ingredients

....

....

....

....

....

....

....

....

Personal Notes:

Directions:

....

....

....

....

....

....

....

....

....

....

Rating: ♧ ♧ ♧ ♧ ♧

Personal Notes:

32 Name:

Date: .... Source: ....

○ Starter ○ Main Course ○ Dessert ○ Baking

Servings: .... Prep Time: .... Cook Time: ....

Difficulty: ○ ○ ○ ○ ○

Ingredients

....
....
....
....
....
....
....
....

Personal Notes:

Directions:

··

··

··

··

··

··

··

··

··

··

··

··

Rating:

Personal Notes:

33 Name:

Date: .... Source: ....

○ Starter ○ Main Course ○ Dessert ○ Baking

Servings: .... Prep Time: .... Cook Time: ....

Difficulty: ○ ○ ○ ○ ○

Ingredients

....
....
....
....
....
....
....
....
....

Personal Notes:

Directions:

....

....

....

....

....

....

....

....

....

....

....

....

Rating:

Personal Notes:

34 Name:

Date: .... Source: ....

○ Starter ○ Main Course ○ Dessert ○ Baking

Servings: .... Prep Time: .... Cook Time: ....

Difficulty: ○ ○ ○ ○ ○

Ingredients

....	....	....	....
....	....	....	....
....	....	....	....
....	....	....	....
....	....	....	....
....	....	....	....
....	....	....	....
....	....	....	....

Personal Notes:

Directions:

....
....
....
....
....
....
....
....
....
....
....
....
....

Rating: ♟ ♟ ♟ ♟ ♟

Personal Notes:

35 Name:

Date: .... Source: ....

○ Starter ○ Main Course ○ Dessert ○ Baking

Servings: .... Prep Time: .... Cook Time: ....

Difficulty: ○ ○ ○ ○ ○

Ingredients

....	....	....	....
....	....	....	....
....	....	....	....
....	....	....	....
....	....	....	....
....	....	....	....
....	....	....	....
....	....	....	....
....	....	....	....

Personal Notes:

Directions:

....

....

....

....

....

....

....

....

....

....

....

Rating: 👨‍🍳 👨‍🍳 👨‍🍳 👨‍🍳 👨‍🍳

Personal Notes:

36 Name: ....

Date: .... Source: ....

○ Starter ○ Main Course ○ Dessert ○ Baking

Servings: .... Prep Time: .... Cook Time: ....

Difficulty: ○ ○ ○ ○ ○

Ingredients

....

....

....

....

....

....

....

....

Personal Notes:

Directions:

....

....

....

....

....

....

....

....

....

....

....

Rating: ♟ ♟ ♟ ♟ ♟

Personal Notes:

37 Name: ....

Date: .... Source: ....

○ Starter ○ Main Course ○ Dessert ○ Baking

Servings: .... Prep Time: .... Cook Time: ....

Difficulty: ○ ○ ○ ○ ○

Ingredients

....

....

....

....

....

....

....

....

Personal Notes:

Directions:

....

....

....

....

....

....

....

....

....

....

Rating: ♟ ♟ ♟ ♟ ♟

Personal Notes:

38 Name: ....

Date: .... Source: ....

○ Starter ○ Main Course ○ Dessert ○ Baking

Servings: .... Prep Time: .... Cook Time: ....

Difficulty: ○ ○ ○ ○ ○

Ingredients

....

....

....

....

....

....

....

....

Personal Notes:

Directions:

....

....

....

....

....

....

....

....

....

....

Rating: ♔ ♔ ♔ ♔ ♔

Personal Notes:

39 Name: ....

Date: .... Source: ....

◯ Starter   ◯ Main Course   ◯ Dessert   ◯ Baking

Servings: .... Prep Time: .... Cook Time: ....

Difficulty: ◯   ◯   ◯   ◯   ◯

Ingredients

....

....

....

....

....

....

....

....

Personal Notes:

Directions:

....

....

....

....

....

....

....

....

....

....

Rating:

Personal Notes:

40 Name: ....

Date: .... Source: ....

○ Starter ○ Main Course ○ Dessert ○ Baking

Servings: .... Prep Time: .... Cook Time: ....

Difficulty: ○ ○ ○ ○ ○

Ingredients

....
....
....
....
....
....
....
....
....

Personal Notes:

Directions:

....

....

....

....

....

....

....

....

....

....

....

Rating:

Personal Notes:

41 Name: ....

Date: .... Source: ....

○ Starter ○ Main Course ○ Dessert ○ Baking

Servings: .... Prep Time: .... Cook Time: ....

Difficulty: ○ ○ ○ ○ ○

Ingredients

....

....

....

....

....

....

....

....

Personal Notes:

Directions:

....

....

....

....

....

....

....

....

....

....

....

Rating: ♟ ♟ ♟ ♟ ♟

Personal Notes:

42 Name: ....

Date: .... Source: ....

○ Starter   ○ Main Course   ○ Dessert   ○ Baking

Servings: .... Prep Time: .... Cook Time: ....

Difficulty: ○   ○   ○   ○   ○

Ingredients

....
....
....
....
....
....
....
....

Personal Notes:

Directions:

Rating: ♙ ♙ ♙ ♙ ♙

Personal Notes:

43 Name:

Date: .... Source: ....

○ Starter ○ Main Course ○ Dessert ○ Baking

Servings: .... Prep Time: .... Cook Time: ....

Difficulty: ○ ○ ○ ○ ○

Ingredients

....
....
....
....
....
....
....
....

Personal Notes:

Directions:

Rating: 🎩 🎩 🎩 🎩 🎩

Personal Notes:

44 Name: ....

Date: .... Source: ....

○ Starter ○ Main Course ○ Dessert ○ Baking

Servings: .... Prep Time: .... Cook Time: ....

Difficulty: ○ ○ ○ ○ ○

Ingredients

....

....

....

....

....

....

....

....

Personal Notes:

Directions:

....

....

....

....

....

....

....

....

....

....

....

....

Rating:

Personal Notes:

45 Name: ....

Date: .... Source: ....

○ Starter ○ Main Course ○ Dessert ○ Baking

Servings: .... Prep Time: .... Cook Time: ....

Difficulty: ○ ○ ○ ○ ○

Ingredients

....
....
....
....
....
....
....
....
....

Personal Notes:

Directions:

....

....

....

....

....

....

....

....

....

....

....

....

Rating:

Personal Notes:

46 **Name:** ....

Date: .... **Source:** ....

○ Starter ○ Main Course ○ Dessert ○ Baking

Servings: .... **Prep Time:** .... **Cook Time:** ....

Difficulty: ○ ○ ○ ○ ○

Ingredients

....

....

....

....

....

....

....

....

....

Personal Notes:

Directions:

....

....

....

....

....

....

....

....

....

....

....

Rating:

Personal Notes:

47 Name: ....

Date: .... Source: ....

○ Starter ○ Main Course ○ Dessert ○ Baking

Servings: .... Prep Time: .... Cook Time: ....

Difficulty: ○ ○ ○ ○ ○

Ingredients

....	....	....	....
....	....	....	....
....	....	....	....
....	....	....	....
....	....	....	....
....	....	....	....
....	....	....	....
....	....	....	....

Personal Notes:

Directions:

Rating: ♟ ♟ ♟ ♟ ♟

Personal Notes:

48 Name:

Date: .... Source: ....

○ Starter ○ Main Course ○ Dessert ○ Baking

Servings: .... Prep Time: .... Cook Time: ....

Difficulty: ○ ○ ○ ○ ○

Ingredients

....

....

....

....

....

....

....

....

Personal Notes:

Directions:

....

....

....

....

....

....

....

....

....

....

....

....

Rating: ♟ ♟ ♟ ♟ ♟

Personal Notes:

49 Name:

Date: .... Source: ....

○ Starter ○ Main Course ○ Dessert ○ Baking

Servings: .... Prep Time: .... Cook Time: ....

Difficulty: ○ ○ ○ ○ ○

Ingredients

....

....

....

....

....

....

....

....

Personal Notes:

Directions:

....

....

....

....

....

....

....

....

....

....

....

....

Rating: ♟ ♟ ♟ ♟ ♟

Personal Notes:

50 Name: ....

Date: .... Source: ....

○ Starter ○ Main Course ○ Dessert ○ Baking

Servings: .... Prep Time: .... Cook Time: ....

Difficulty: ○ ○ ○ ○ ○

Ingredients

....

....

....

....

....

....

....

....

Personal Notes:

Directions:

....

....

....

....

....

....

....

....

....

....

....

Rating:

Personal Notes:

 |||

51 Name:

Date: .... Source: ....

○ Starter ○ Main Course ○ Dessert ○ Baking

Servings: .... Prep Time: .... Cook Time: ....

Difficulty: ○ ○ ○ ○ ○

Ingredients

....

....

....

....

....

....

....

....

Personal Notes:

Directions:

....

....

....

....

....

....

....

....

....

....

....

Rating: ♟ ♟ ♟ ♟ ♟

Personal Notes:

52 Name: ....

Date: .... Source: ....

○ Starter   ○ Main Course   ○ Dessert   ○ Baking

Servings: .... Prep Time: .... Cook Time: ....

Difficulty: ○   ○   ○   ○   ○

Ingredients

....

....

....

....

....

....

....

....

....

Personal Notes:

Directions:

....

....

....

....

....

....

....

....

....

....

....

....

Rating: ♙ ♙ ♙ ♙ ♙

Personal Notes:

53 Name:

Date: .... Source: ....

○ Starter ○ Main Course ○ Dessert ○ Baking

Servings: .... Prep Time: .... Cook Time: ....

Difficulty: ○ ○ ○ ○ ○

Ingredients

....	....	....	....
....	....	....	....
....	....	....	....
....	....	....	....
....	....	....	....
....	....	....	....
....	....	....	....
....	....	....	....
....	....	....	....

Personal Notes:

Directions:

....

....

....

....

....

....

....

....

....

....

....

Rating: ♙ ♙ ♙ ♙ ♙

Personal Notes:

54 Name:

Date: .... Source: ....

○ Starter ○ Main Course ○ Dessert ○ Baking

Servings: .... Prep Time: .... Cook Time: ....

Difficulty: ○ ○ ○ ○ ○

Ingredients

....

....

....

....

....

....

....

....

Personal Notes:

Directions:

....

....

....

....

....

....

....

....

....

....

....

....

Rating: ♕ ♕ ♕ ♕ ♕

Personal Notes:

55 Name:

Date: .... Source: ....

○ Starter   ○ Main Course   ○ Dessert   ○ Baking

Servings: .... Prep Time: .... Cook Time: ....

Difficulty: ○   ○   ○   ○   ○

Ingredients

....

....

....

....

....

....

....

....

Personal Notes:

Directions:

Rating: ♙ ♙ ♙ ♙ ♙

Personal Notes:

56 Name: ....

Date: .... Source: ....

○ Starter   ○ Main Course   ○ Dessert   ○ Baking

Servings: .... Prep Time: .... Cook Time: ....

Difficulty: ○   ○   ○   ○   ○

Ingredients

....

....

....

....

....

....

....

....

....

Personal Notes:

Directions:

....

....

....

....

....

....

....

....

....

....

Rating:

Personal Notes:

57

Name: ....

Date: .... **Source:** ....

○ Starter ○ Main Course ○ Dessert ○ Baking

Servings: .... **Prep Time:** .... **Cook Time:** ....

Difficulty: ○ ○ ○ ○ ○

Ingredients

....

....

....

....

....

....

....

....

....

Personal Notes:

Directions:

....

....

....

....

....

....

....

....

....

....

....

Rating: ♟ ♟ ♟ ♟ ♟

Personal Notes:

58 Name: ....

Date: .... Source: ....

○ Starter ○ Main Course ○ Dessert ○ Baking

Servings: .... Prep Time: .... Cook Time: ....

Difficulty: ○   ○   ○   ○   ○

Ingredients

....
....
....
....
....
....
....
....
....

Personal Notes:

Directions:

Rating: 🎩 🎩 🎩 🎩 🎩

Personal Notes:

59 Name:

Date: .... Source: ....

○ Starter ○ Main Course ○ Dessert ○ Baking

Servings: .... Prep Time: .... Cook Time: ....

Difficulty: ○ ○ ○ ○ ○

Ingredients

....

....

....

....

....

....

....

....

Personal Notes:

Directions:

....

....

....

....

....

....

....

....

....

....

....

Rating:

Personal Notes:

60 Name: ....

Date: .... Source: ....

○ Starter ○ Main Course ○ Dessert ○ Baking

Servings: .... Prep Time: .... Cook Time: ....

Difficulty: ○ ○ ○ ○ ○

Ingredients

....

....

....

....

....

....

....

....

....

Personal Notes:

Directions:

....

....

....

....

....

....

....

....

....

....

....

Rating: ♟ ♟ ♟ ♟ ♟

Personal Notes:

61 Name:

Date: .... Source: ....

○ Starter ○ Main Course ○ Dessert ○ Baking

Servings: .... Prep Time: .... Cook Time: ....

Difficulty: ○ ○ ○ ○ ○

Ingredients

....	....	....	....
....	....	....	....
....	....	....	....
....	....	....	....
....	....	....	....
....	....	....	....
....	....	....	....
....	....	....	....

Personal Notes:

Directions:

....
....
....
....
....
....
....
....
....
....

Rating:

Personal Notes:

62 Name: ....

Date: .... Source: ....

○ Starter ○ Main Course ○ Dessert ○ Baking

Servings: .... Prep Time: .... Cook Time: ....

Difficulty: ○ ○ ○ ○ ○

Ingredients

....

....

....

....

....

....

....

....

....

Personal Notes:

Directions:

....

....

....

....

....

....

....

....

....

....

....

Rating: ♙ ♙ ♙ ♙ ♙

Personal Notes:

63 Name: ....

Date: .... Source: ....

○ Starter ○ Main Course ○ Dessert ○ Baking

Servings: .... Prep Time: .... Cook Time: ....

Difficulty: ○ ○ ○ ○ ○

Ingredients

....

....

....

....

....

....

....

....

Personal Notes:

Directions:

....

....

....

....

....

....

....

....

....

....

....

Rating: ♟ ♟ ♟ ♟ ♟

Personal Notes:

64 Name: ....

Date: .... Source: ....

○ Starter ○ Main Course ○ Dessert ○ Baking

Servings: .... Prep Time: .... Cook Time: ....

Difficulty: ○ ○ ○ ○ ○

Ingredients

....

....

....

....

....

....

....

....

....

Personal Notes:

Directions:

....

....

....

....

....

....

....

....

....

....

Rating: ♟ ♟ ♟ ♟ ♟

Personal Notes: